WAR MACHINES

SUBMARINES

by
David West

CRABTREE
PUBLISHING COMPANY
WWW.CRABTREEBOOKS.COM

CRABTREE
PUBLISHING COMPANY
WWW.CRABTREEBOOKS.COM

Author and designer: David West

Illustrator: David West

Editorial director: Kathy Middleton

Editor: Ellen Rodger

Proofreader: Melissa Boyce

**Production coordinator
and Prepress technician**: Ken Wright

Print coordinator: Katherine Berti

Library and Archives Canada Cataloguing in Publication

Title: Submarines / David West.
Names: West, David, 1956- author.
Description: Series statement: War machines | Includes index.
Identifiers: Canadiana (print) 20190105763 |
    Canadiana (print) 20190106859 |
    Canadiana (ebook) 20190106859 |
    ISBN 9780778766681 (hardcover) |
    ISBN 9780778766834 (softcover) |
    ISBN 9781427124104 (HTML)
Subjects: LCSH: Submarines (Ships)—Juvenile literature.
Classification: LCC VM365 .W47 2019 | j623.825/7—dc23

Library of Congress Cataloging-in-Publication Data

Names: West, David, 1956- author.
Title: Submarines / David West.
Description: New York : Crabtree Publishing Company, [2019]
    Series: War machines | Includes index. |
    Audience: Grades 7-8. | Audience: Ages 10-14 and up. |
Identifiers: LCCN 2019014230 (print) |
    LCCN 2019015894 (ebook) |
    ISBN 9781427124104 (Electronic) |
    ISBN 9780778766681 (hardcover) |
    ISBN 9780778766834 (pbk.)
Subjects: LCSH: Submarines (Ships)--Juvenile literature.
Classification: LCC VM365 (ebook) |
    LCC VM365 .W474 2019 (print) | DDC 623.825/7--dc23
LC record available at https://lccn.loc.gov/2019014230

Crabtree Publishing Company
www.crabtreebooks.com   1-800-387-7650

Published by Crabtree Publishing Company in 2020

Project development, design, and concept:
David West Children's Books

Printed in the U.S.A./072019/CG20190501

Published in Canada
Crabtree Publishing
616 Welland Ave.
St. Catharines, ON
L2M 5V6

Published in the United States
Crabtree Publishing
PMB 59051, 350 Fifth Ave.
59th Floor,
New York, NY

Contents

Submarines

The first military submarines could only travel for short distances while underwater. During **World War I** (1914–1918), submarines were made with sturdy double hulls—an outer hull and an inner hull called a pressure hull. The pressure hull had **ballast tanks** that could be filled with air or water to make them rise or sink. To steer while diving underwater, the subs used movable short wings at the stern, or back, called hydroplanes. A conning tower, also called a fin or sail, helped to keep the submarine stable. It housed sensors, as well as periscopes for looking around and above objects. Batteries powered the sub's electric motors while submerged. By the end of **World War II** (1939–1945), submarines spent most of their time at the surface. In the 1950s, **nuclear power** allowed subs to stay underwater longer. Modern submarines (SSBNs) have become large platforms for nuclear **ballistic missiles**. Others, called hunter-killers (SSNs), are designed to destroy SSBNs.

This Japanese Sōryū-class diesel-electric fast attack submarine uses Stirling engines. These engines do not need air for pressure to help the sub remain submerged for long periods of time.

Early Submarines

The first military submarine was built in 1720 by Russian carpenter Yefim Nikonov. It looked like a giant wooden barrel. Built for Russian **Czar** Peter the Great, it was armed with flamethrowers. Unfortunately, it sank during its first trial in 1724.

Many successful human-powered submarines were built around the world. American inventor Robert Fulton made the *Nautilus* for the French Navy in 1800. Jose Rodriguez Lavandera created the

On February 17, 1864, the Confederate States of America launched the *Hunley* on a mission to sink a warship, the USS *Housatonic*. The mission was successful, but the *Hunley* sank before it could return to base. All the crew were lost.

Hipopotamo for the Ecuadorian Navy in 1837. Neither was very successful. The first submarine to successfully sink a ship was the *H. L. Hunley*. This submarine used explosives attached to a wooden spar that was 22 feet (6.7 m) long, mounted on the *Hunley*'s bow. Seven crew members turned a crank handle to power the propeller, while one person steered.

The *Turtle*, designed by David Bushnell, was the first American military submarine. It was built in 1775 and was used during the **American Revolutionary War** (1775–1783).

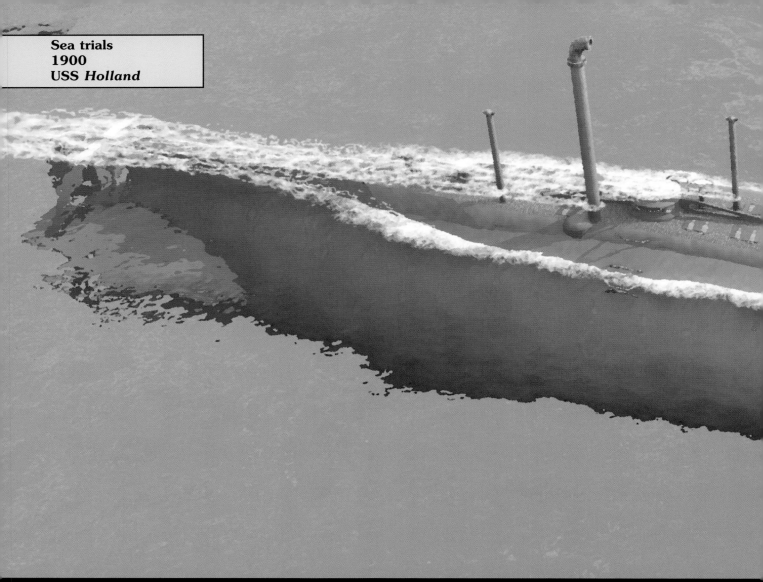

The Modern Sub

The first submarine to fire a torpedo was the _Abdülhamid_ in 1887. It was built in England by Thorsten Nordenfelt, a Swedish inventor. It was powered by a steam engine which shut down when it dove. Electric **propulsion** for traveling underwater was only possible after the invention of the electric battery.

The **internal combustion engine** made the submarine more useful. Powered by a gas or diesel engine while on the surface, an electric

8

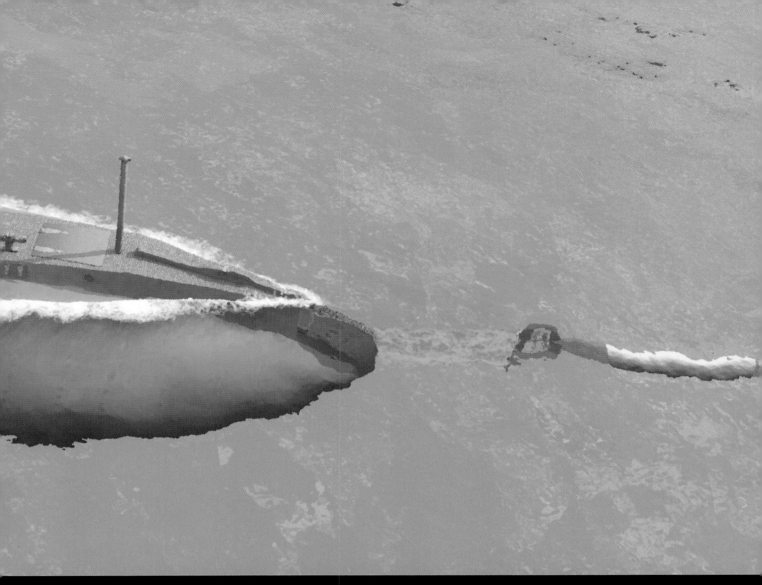

The USS *Holland* fires a torpedo during trials in 1900. It had many of the features of today's modern subs, such as a periscope, internal combustion engine, electric motor, and torpedo tubes, as well as ballast and trim tanks to change position underwater.

motor powered by batteries was used when underwater. Launched in 1897, the USS *Holland* was soon bought by the United States and became the United States Navy's first submarine. Holland submarines were also bought by Britain's Royal Navy.

The self-propelled torpedo was invented by Robert Whitehead in 1866. It was this weapon that made navies around the world see the potential of the submarine.

WWI Submarines

By the beginning of World War I (WWI), the Imperial German Navy and Great Britain's Royal Navy had the largest submarine fleets. Most of the early military submarines were powered by a diesel engine while on the surface. They used a battery-powered electric motor when submerged.

These early submarines were armed with torpedoes and many had cannons attached to their decks. Some were armed with **mines** which

10

U-20 surfaces after torpedoing the RMS *Lusitania* on May 7, 1915, off the southern coast of Ireland. In total, 1,198 passengers and crew died, including 128 American citizens. The sinking helped shift public opinion in the United States against Germany.

hey could lay in busy shipping lanes without detection. As the British fleet remained in control at sea, German submarines, known as U-boats, attacked commercial and naval ships. The U-boat attacks were very damaging. The sinking of the passenger liner *Lusitania* in 1915 and the oss of American lives was one of the reasons the U.S. decided o enter the war in 1917.

U-21 was a typical U-boat. In September 1914, it became the first submarine to sink a ship with a self-propelled torpedo. It destroyed the cruiser HMS *Pathfinder* in the North Sea.

Aircraft-Carrying Subs

Many countries experimented with submarine aircraft carriers between the wars. Most were built during World War II (WWII). Japan built more than anyone else.

The aircraft carried by these submarines were for **reconnaissance**, but some were **bombers** that could carry torpedoes as well. The I-400-class submarine built by the Imperial Japanese Navy carried three Aichi M6A Seiran aircraft. These were held in a special watertight hanger. It took a crew of four 30 minutes to prepare and launch all three aircraft.

12

During trials off the coast of Japan near the end of WWII, a Japanese I-400-class submarine launches two Aichi M6A Seiran floatplanes. The floatplanes were sent up into the air via a deck-mounted catapult.

At 400 feet (122 m) long, these submarines were the largest of WWII, and remained the largest until nuclear missile subs were built in the 1960s. The I-400 class could only dive to a depth of 328 feet (100 m). Their size meant they were easily found and destroyed by enemy ships and planes.

The fight against submarines during both world wars created a need for flying boats such as the Consolidated PBY Catalina. They were the most numerous of the antisubmarine aircraft in both the Atlantic and Pacific Oceans. They destroyed 40 submarines during WWII.

U-boats of WWII

During WWII, the Kriegsmarine (German War Navy) produced many different types of U-boats. The Type 7 U-boats were the most common. Larger Type 9 boats were designed for long-range patrols. Some of these traveled as far as Japan and the United States.

Early on, U-boats hunted in wolfpacks. These were groups of three U-boats that worked together to destroy ships in **Allied convoys** in the Atlantic Ocean. This was known as the **Battle of the Atlantic**.

14

U-boat *U-201* is attacked by 99 depth charges from three Allied escort ships during the Battle of the Atlantic. Although *severely* damaged, it escaped. On a later patrol in 1943, *U-201* was destroyed by a British warship just east of the Canadian coast.

WWII subs spent most of their time on the surface, diving down to hunt and attack. Their main weapon was the torpedo and the element of surprise. Deck guns were also used on the surface. Later, Allied ships used underwater sound detection to find submerged U-boats and destroy them with **depth charges**.

The Type 21 and 23 "Elektroboot" were designed to operate submerged for most of the time. They used batteries to increase the time spent underwater. Elektroboots would surface to periscope depth to recharge.

15

Human Torpedoes

Torpedoes were small submarines deployed to sink ships in harbors. They were both manned and unmanned. The first human torpedo was the Italian Maiale, which made many raids in the Mediterranean.

The Maiale was propelled by an electric motor and piloted by two crew in diving suits. After being carried close to their destination by a larger submarine, the crew boarded the torpedo and steered at slow speed to the enemy ship. The warhead was detached and placed under the ship

16

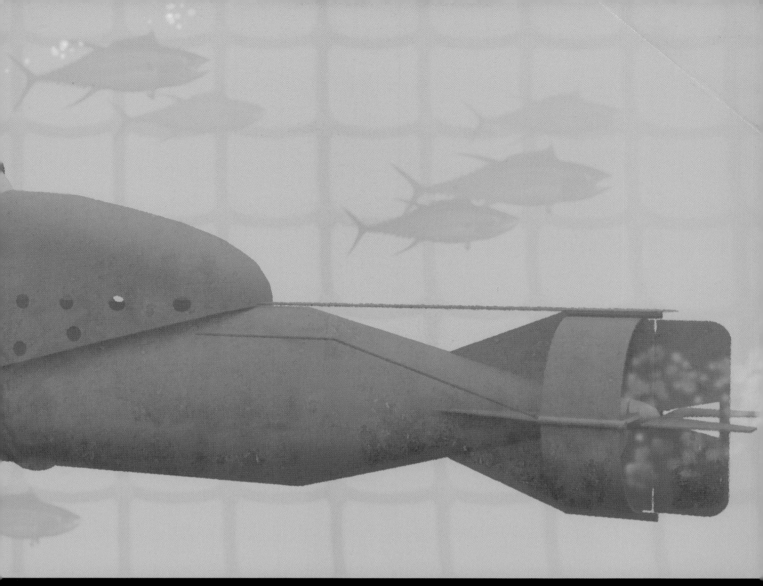

One of three Italian Maiale-type human torpedoes maneuvers past an antisubmarine net at the mouth of the harbor of Alexandria. Two British battleships, HMS *Queen Elizabeth* and HMS *Valiant*, and the tanker *Sagona* were damaged.

with a time fuse. The crew then rode the torpedo away. The British Royal Navy copied the designs and named them Chariots. The Japanese Imperial Navy's Kaiten was a manned torpedo used as a suicide weapon. Pilots were locked into the torpedos as they hit their targets.

The German Kriegsmarine's Neger human torpedo was deployed at night because it could not submerge. The single pilot aimed the craft at the target and released the torpedo before steering away.

Midget Submarines

Midget submarines were small submarines that normally had a two-person crew. They were very cramped inside. Midget submarines were usually launched and recovered by a "mother" ship or sub, since they could only travel short distances.

During WWII, most midget submarines, such as the British X-Craft, were used to penetrate harbors and sink ships inside them. Torpedoes were fired or divers would attach **limpet mines** to enemy vessels. Germany's

18

A German Kriegsmarine Seehund-class midget submarine prepares to fire one of its two torpedoes at a cargo ship off the coast of southeast England during WWII.

Seehund midget subs had a large enough range to attack ships off the southeast coast of England. They could dive to a depth of 148 feet (45 m). Seehunds were deployed late in the war and were used against the Allied invasion of Europe and to disrupt supply lines.

The Type A Ko-hyoteki class of Japanese midget submarines were used during WWII to attack ships in Pearl Harbor, Sydney Harbor, and during the Battle of Madagascar in 1942.

578

Nuclear Power

The first nuclear-powered submarine, the USS *Nautilus*, was launched in 1954. Its power source was a **nuclear reactor**, so it never needed refueling and could stay submerged for long periods of time. It just needed to carry enough food to feed the crew on long hauls.

The Skate-class submarines were based on the USS *Nautilus*. These were the first nuclear-powered submarines of the U.S. Navy. The USS *Skate* was the first in the class. It was smaller than the *Nautilus*.

The USS *Skate* succeeds in surfacing through the Arctic Ocean's thick ice at the North Pole on March 17, 1959. It was the *Skate*'s second attempt to surface at the pole. The first was in August 1958, but the ice was too thick to safely break through.

Like the *Nautilus,* it made several trips under the Arctic ice. It was designed so that it could break through the ice to surface. In 1959, it became the first submarine to surface at the North Pole. The Skate-class subs were retired from service in the 1980s.

The USS *Nautilus* broke many records. In 1958, it became the first submarine to travel under the Arctic ice and pass under the North Pole. It was designed as a fast attack submarine, but was never used in combat.

21

Ballistic Missile Subs

Nuclear-powered ballistic missile submarines (SSBNs) are large, underwater missile platforms designed to stay hidden in the world's oceans. Their missiles can travel more than 3,418 miles (5,500 km).

SSBNs have to be good at hiding. They have devices to dampen vibrating machinery and a special skin that makes it difficult for sonar to detect them. Sonar uses sound vibration to find and determine the distance of objects. Active sonar sends out sounds, or "pings." If a ping

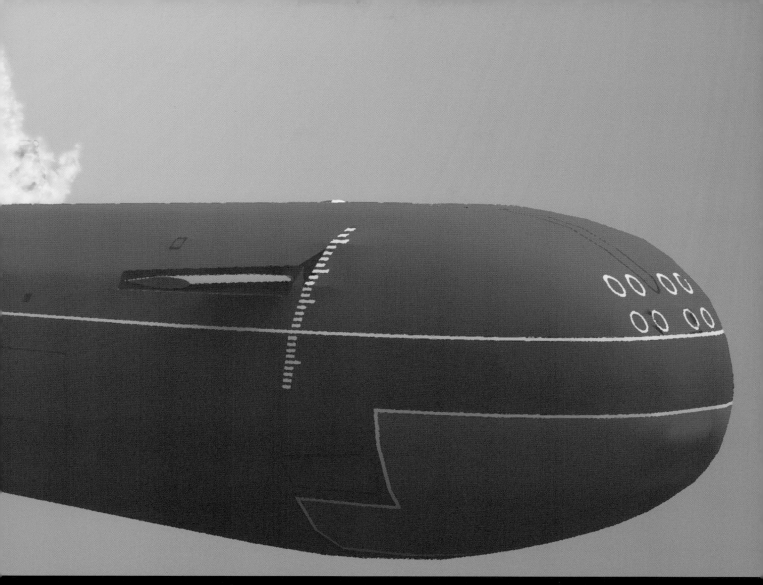

A Soviet Typhoon-class ballistic missile submarine test-fires an R-39 Rif SLBM (Submarine-Launched Ballistic Missile) from beneath the ocean's surface. It carries 20 SLBMs as well as cruise missiles and torpedoes.

bounces back, it has hit an object such as another sub. SSBNs also use passive sonar. It detects things without sending out a ping. The first SSBNs were built during the **Cold War** (1947–1991). The **Soviet Union**'s Typhoon-class subs were the largest ever built. The **missile silos** were in front of the central fin, and it had two inner hulls, with a third on top. Typhoons could stay submerged for more than 120 days.

The Ohio-class SSBN carries 24 Trident SLBMs in tubes behind the central fin.

Hunter-Killers

Hunter-killer or fast attack submarines are designed to hunt and destroy enemy submarines and surface ships. Some lay mines. They can also destroy targets on land by launching Tomahawk **cruise missiles**.

Nuclear-powered fast attack submarines are known as SSNs. Some, like the U.S. Virginia class, transport special operations forces such as **Navy SEALS** to carry out missions on land. The latest SSNs use jump-jet propulsors, a mechanical device that produces a jet of water to propel a

The USS *North Dakota* is a Virginia-class fast attack submarine. Here, it test launches a Tomahawk cruise missile from one of its two forward vertical launch tubes.

sub through water. Propulsors are quieter than propellers, which can be picked up by an enemy submarine's passive sonar. Passive sonar listens without transmitting, so the submarine's position is not revealed.

Diesel-electric fast attack submarines are quieter than nuclear-powered submarines. This Japanese Navy Sōryū−class submarine is almost silent.

Rescue Submarines

Deep Submergence Rescue Vehicles (DSRVs) are designed to rescue crew from damaged submarines. DSRVs are flown to the nearest port. From there, they are carried to the stricken submarine by a surface support ship or "mother" submarine (MOSUB).

DSRVs can rescue up to 24 people at a time, at depths of up to 4,921 feet (1,500 m). A DSRV can **maneuver** into position using its four thrusters. Then it can dock over an escape hatch situated on top of the

The Deep-Submergence Rescue Vehicle *Mystic* dives towards a Los Angeles-class submarine during a simulated submarine rescue mission.

submarine near the conning tower. People rescued from the stranded sub are transferred to the support ship. There are three spheres inside the DSRV. The pilot and copilot operate the vehicle in the front sphere. The other two spheres are used for the rescued crew.

The Oscar-class submarine *Kursk* (shown here) sank during a Russian naval exercise in 2000. All 118 people on board died. Since then, navies around the world cooperate in rescuing crews from downed submarines.

Special Operations

The **stealth** capabilities of modern submarines are ideal for secret operations in enemy waters. During the Cold War, some submarines were outfitted with spy gear.

In the early 1970s, the United States sent the USS *Halibut* to the Pacific Ocean north of Japan. The *Halibut* was a nuclear-powered guided missile submarine (SSGN) retooled as a spy sub. Divers from the *Halibut* attached a listening device to a Soviet underwater communications cable.

The USS *Parche* was a modified Sturgeon-class submarine. Divers for the *Parche* are shown here retrieving recordings from a Soviet underwater communications line. The spying exercise, called wiretapping, took place on the ocean floor off the coast of Russia.

Submarines such as the USS *Parche* later retrieved and replaced tapes from the listening device. Other operations included picking up ballistic missile fragments from the seabed. These came from Soviet and Chinese test launches.

The *Belgorod*, a modified OSCAR II cruise missile submarine, is the latest Russian spy sub platform. It carries a nuclear-powered midget sub that will be used to build a military complex in the Arctic.

Submarine Specs

More information about the submarines in this book

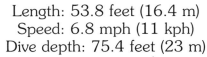

Holland
Length: 53.8 feet (16.4 m)
Speed: 6.8 mph (11 kph)
Dive depth: 75.4 feet (23 m)

U-20
Length: 210.6 feet (64.2 m)
Speed: 17.7 mph (28.5 kph)
Dive depth: 164 feet (50 m)

Hunley
Length: 39.3 feet (12 m)
Speed: 4.6 mph (7.4 kph)
Dive depth: A few feet

I-400 class
Length: 400.3 feet (122 m)
Speed: 21.5 mph (34.6 kph)
Dive depth: 330 feet (100 m)

U-201
Length: 219.8 feet (67 m)
Speed: 20.4 mph (32.8 kph)
Dive depth: 754.5 feet (230 m)

Seehund
Length: 39.4 feet (12 m)
Speed: 8 mph (13 kph)
Dive depth: 148 feet (45 m)

Maiale-type manned torpedo
Length: 16.4 feet (5 m)
Speed: 5 mph (8 kph)
Dive depth: 98.4 feet (30 m)

USS Skate
Length: 267.4 feet (81.5 m)
Speed: 20.5 mph (33 kph)
Dive depth: 689 feet (210 m)

USS North Dakota
Length: 377.3 feet (115 m)
Speed: 28.6 mph (46 kph)
Dive depth: 787.4 feet (240 m)

Typhoon-class SSBN
Length: 574 feet (175 m)
Speed: 31 mph (50 kph)
Dive depth: 1,312.3 feet (400 m)

DSRV Mystic
Length: 49 feet (15 m)
Speed: 4.6 mph (7.4 kph)
Dive depth: 4,921.3 feet (1,500 m)

USS Parche
Length: 400.3 feet (122 m)
Speed: 28.6 mph (46 kph)
Dive depth: 1,299.2 feet (396 m)

Glossary

Allied convoys Groups of merchant ships that carried goods and people from the United Kingdom to North America during World War II. They sailed together for safety against German U-boat attacks.

American Revolutionary War (1775–1783) The war between Great Britain and its Thirteen Colonies which declared independence as the United States of America

ballast tanks Compartments within a sub that are filled with water or air to make it sink or float. The submarine can be made to go up or down, depending on which tanks are used.

ballistic missiles Missiles with high, arching trajectories

Battle of the Atlantic (1939–1945) The longest continuous military campaign of WWII, where German U-boats and the Luftwaffe air force were pitted against the British Royal Navy, Royal Canadian Navy, Allied merchant ships, and later, the United States Navy

bombers A military aircraft that drops bombs

Cold War (1947–1991) The name of the politically hostile relationship between the United States and the Soviet Union after World War II

cruise missiles Low-flying missiles that are guided to their target by a computer

Czar Russian emperor or ruler

depth charges Antisubmarine weapons that explode at a specific depth of water, destroying or disabling a sub

internal combustion engine An engine that burns fuel such as gas or diesel, with air inside the engine

limpet mine An explosive device that can be attached to the metal hull of a ship using magnets

maneuver To move skillfully or carefully

mines Explosive devices placed in water to destroy or damage ships and subs

missile silo A cylindrical structure from which a submarine-launched ballistic missile is launched

Navy SEALS A special operations force of the U.S. Navy, made up of Sea, Air, and Land teams

nuclear power The use of atomic energy in a reactor to create heat, which produces steam to drive turbines for power

nuclear reactor A device that uses thermal energy from a controlled nuclear reaction to create power to run subs

propulsion The action of driving something forward

reconnaissance A search made by military forces of an area to get information about the positions, numbers, and equipment of enemy forces

Soviet Union (1922–1991) A former union of states in Eastern Europe and Asia

stealth Difficult to detect by sight, sound, radar, or other means

World War I (1914–1918) An international conflict fought mainly in Europe and the Middle East, between the Central powers, including Austria-Hungary, Germany, and the Ottoman Empire, and the Allies, including the United Kingdom, Canada, Australia, and later, the United States

World War II (1939–1945) An international conflict fought in Europe, Asia, and Africa, between the Axis powers, including Germany, Italy, and Japan, and the Allies, including the United Kingdom, France, Canada, Australia, and in 1941, the United States

Index